Logic Mysteries for Young Readers

"GRID" PUZZLES FOR GRADES 2–4

	Canary	Hamster	Turtle	Pony
Emma	✗	✗	✗	✔
Jacob	✗	✔	✗	✗
Zoe	✔	✗	✗	✗
Hunter	✗	✗	✔	✗

Written By Rebecca Stark
Illustrated by Karen Birchak

Educational Books 'n' Bingo

I0155798

The purchase of this book entitles the individual teacher to reproduce copies of the student pages for use in his or her classroom exclusively. The reproduction of any part of the work for an entire school or school system or for commercial use is prohibited.

ISBN: 978-1-56644-535-1

© 2016 Barbara M. Peller, also known as Rebecca Stark

Printed in the United States of America.

Table of Contents

To the Teacher

These logic problems were designed to improve students' deductive-reasoning and other critical-thinking skills. They also improve memory and reading-comprehension skills and encourage students to expand their vocabularies. The logic mysteries are divided into three levels, with Level 1 containing the easiest problems and Level 3 containing the most difficult. A template for students to create their own logic mysteries is also provided.

Students should work on most of these mysteries alone, in pairs, or in small groups. Groups can compete against each other to see which group can solve the problem first. You may also want to do a few on the board as a whole-class activity. In this case it is probably best not to give students their own copies. Instead, have students listen carefully and perhaps jot down a note or two as you read the story and the clues. As an extra challenge, do a few without filling in the matrix on the board. Students must listen carefully and try to remember the information in the story and the clues! You will probably want to start with easier ones for this option. Another option is to have students take a problem home to do as a family activity.

Students should read the introduction to each mystery carefully. Explain that some of the information given here may be needed to solve the mystery. Instruct students to use context clues to figure out any new vocabulary words which appear and to use their dictionaries if they still aren't sure of the meaning.

The following should be kept in mind as students work on these mysteries:
- Names that are usually girls' names can be assumed to be girls' names.
- Names that are usually boys' names can be assumed to be boys' names.
- It is sometimes necessary to re-read the introduction. There may be important information not repeated in the clues.
- Some clues may not be used to solve the mystery.
- Some clues may be useful later on when more facts are known.
- A matrix (grid) helps organize the information.
- It sometimes helps to make a diagram or chart.

COMMON CORE STATE STANDARDS: ANCHOR STANDARDS FOR READING

Key Ideas and Details:
CCSS.ELA-LITERACY.CCRA.R.1
Read closely to determine what the text says explicitly and to make logical inferences from it; cite specific textual evidence when writing or speaking to support conclusions drawn from the text.

NOTE: A Hints for Solving Logic Mysteries sheet is provided for duplication.

 © Barbara M. Peller

Instructions:

Read the introduction carefully. It might have important information not repeated in the clues. As you read each clue, keep track of what you learn by filling in the matrix whenever you can. Remember, not all clues will help you solve the mystery. When a choice can be eliminated, fill in the space on the grid with an ✗. When a choice can be substantiated, fill in the space on the grid with a ✔. Fill in the rest of the spaces down and across with an ✗ (unless you have been given information that says otherwise).

Which Pet?

Three kids named Marla, Joe, and Sara each have a different pet. The pets are a canary, a hamster, and a goldfish.

Which kid has which pet?

Clues

1. Marla's pet is a not a mammal.

2. Joe's pet has no fins.

3. Sara's pet has feathers.

Using the Matrix

1. The first clue tells us that Marla's pet is a not a mammal. Because the hamster is a mammal, we put an ✗ in the place on the grid where Marla and hamster meet.

2. The second clue tells us that Joe's pet has no fins. Because only fish have fins, we put an ✗ in the place on the grid where Joe and fish meet.

3. The third clue tells us that Sara's pet has feathers. Because the canary is a bird and, therefore, has feathers, we put a ✔ in the place on the grid where Sara and canary meet. We also put an ✗ where Sara and the other 2 pets meet and where Joe and Marla meet the canary.

Now we also know that Joe has to have the hamster and Marla has to have the fish!

GRID AFTER FIRST CLUE

	Canary	Hamster	Fish
Marla		✗	
Joe			
Sara			

GRID AFTER SECOND CLUE

	Canary	Hamster	Fish
Marla		✗	
Joe			✗
Sara			

GRID AFTER THIRD CLUE

	Canary	Hamster	Fish
Marla	✗	✗	
Joe	✗		✗
Sara	✔	✗	✗

	Canary	Hamster	Fish
Marla	✗	✗	✔
Joe	✗	✔	✗
Sara	✔	✗	✗

© Barbara M. Peller

Hints for Solving Logic Mysteries

Keep the following in mind when solving these logic problems.

1. Names that are usually girls' names can be assumed to be girls' names unless otherwise stated.

2. Names that are usually boys' names can be assumed to be boys' names unless otherwise stated.

3. It is sometimes necessary to reread the introduction. There may be important information not repeated in the clues.

4. Some clues may not be necessary for solving the mystery.

5. Some clues may be misleading; for example, just because someone likes something does not necessarily mean that he or she chose it at the particular time in question.

6. Some clues may be useful later on when more information is given. This applies to clues you have used to gain other important information as well as to those that have not yet been useful.

7. A matrix (grid) helps organize the information.

8. It sometimes helps to draw a diagram (for example, a seating chart).

9. Jot down notes as necessary.

10. Remember, once a choice can be substantiated, you can *usually* eliminate the other choices.

© **Barbara M. Peller**

Level 1 Mysteries

© Barbara M. Peller

Scoops for You

Scoops for You, an ice-cream parlor with more than forty flavors of ice cream, just opened near Maplewood Elementary School. All of the children were very excited about its opening. Four of those children—Becca, Eli, Jennie, and Carolina—made plans to visit the ice-cream parlor after school.

At 3:15 the four friends met in the school playground and together walked to Scoops for You. They studied the flavor chart carefully and then they placed their orders. Three of them wanted ice-cream cones: one of the three ordered a single scoop, one ordered a double scoop, and one ordered a triple scoop. The child who ordered the single scoop asked for cookie dough. The one who ordered the double scoop requested banana and chocolate. The child who ordered the triple scoop wanted vanilla, chocolate, and chocolate chip. The fourth child requested an ice-cream sundae made with strawberry ice cream and chocolate syrup.

Use the clues and the information given above to figure out what each child ordered.

Clues

1. Jennie is allergic to chocolate.

2. Eli and the child who ordered the ice-cream cone with the most scoops were cousins.

3. The color of the ice cream ordered by the girl whose name has four syllables can be made by mixing red and white paint.

© **Barbara M. Peller**

Matrix for Scoops for You

	1 Scoop	2 Scoops	3 Scoops	Sundae
Becca				
Eli				
Jennie				
Carolina				

Becca ordered _____.

Eric ordered _____.

Jenn ordered _____.

Carolina ordered _____.

Which Sport?

Fourth graders Ethan, Jacob, Andrew, and Austin have been friends since they were in kindergarten together. They have a lot in common, including the fact that all four of them are interested in sports. Each friend, however, favors a different sport. The sports they favor are soccer, basketball, baseball, and field hockey.

Use the clues to figure out each child's favorite sport.

Clues

1. The boy whose name has the most vowels never played field hockey.

2. The name of the boy whose favorite sport involves the use of a bat comes third alphabetically.

3. Jacob is older than the boy who favors soccer and younger than the boy who favors field hockey.

© **Barbara M. Peller**

Matrix for Which Sport?

	Soccer	Basketball	Baseball	Field Hockey
Ethan				
Jacob				
Andrew				
Austin				

Ethan favors _____.

Jacob favors _____.

Andrew favors _____.

Austin favors _____.

© Barbara M. Peller

A Foul-Shooting Competition

The fifth-grade class at Woodlawn Elementary School held a foul-shooting contest. The top four contestants were Brad, Justin, Rebecca, and Zack. Their last names were Apple, Black, Green, and Rose. Each student was told to take 25 foul shots. The number of shots they made were 17, 19, 20, and 23.

Use the clues and the information in the introduction to figure out their last names and which child got each score.

Clues

1. Justin made two fewer shots than the boy whose last name is the name of a fruit.

2. The name of the kid who shot one more than the kid named Apple is the name of a color.

3. The last name of the kid who made 20 shots rhymes with his first name.

4. The girl named Green shot six more than the boy whose name is also the name of a flower.

© **Barbara M. Peller**

Matrix for A Foul-Shooting Competition

	Apple	Black	Green	Rose	17	19	20	23
Brad								
Justin								
Rebecca								
Zack								

Brad _____ made _____ shots.

Justin _____ made _____ shots.

Rebecca _____ made _____ shots.

Zack _____ made _____ shots.

_____ won the competition.

© Barbara M. Peller

The Oakville Town Fair Puzzle Contest

Every year as part of the Oakville Town Fair, a Jigsaw Puzzle Contest was held. There were four different age groups: Grades K–2, Grades 3–5, Grades 6–8, and Grades 9–12. Members of each group were given the same puzzle. Whoever finished the group's puzzle first would be the winner of that group.

This year, when the contest ended, Scarlet, Brianna, Jimmy, and Rebecca were the four winners. All four children were very excited! Not only was the mayor going to award them with trophies, but their names and pictures would also appear in the local newspaper as part of an article describing the event!

Use the clues and the information in the introduction to figure out who won each group.

Clues

1. Jimmy is in a different group this year than last year.

2. The winner of the oldest group often babysat for the winner of the youngest group.

3. The boy was not in the oldest group.

4. Brianna and the winner of the oldest group met for the first time on the day of the Town Fair.

5. The name of the winner of the youngest group is the only name without a double letter.

6. Last year Jimmy won in the Grades 3–5 Group.

     © **Barbara M. Peller**

Matrix for The Oakville Town Fair Puzzle Contest

	Grades K-2	Grades 3-5	Grades 6-8	Grades 9-12
Scarlet				
Brianna				
Jimmy				
Rebecca				

Scarlet was the winner of the _____ Group.

Brianna was the winner of the _____ Group.

Jimmy was the winner of the _____ Group.

Rebecca was the winner of the _____ Group.

Works of Art!

The winners of the Oakville Town Fair Puzzle Contest were announced in the *Oakville News* as promised. The article informed readers that Scarlet was the winner of the Grades K–2 Group, Brianna was the winner of the Grades 3–5 Group, Jimmy was the winner of the Grades 6–8 Group, and Rebecca was the winner of the Grades 9–12 Group. It listed the names of the puzzles: "Jungle Scene," "A Day at the Beach," "Playground Fun," and "Animal Babies."

The reporter congratulated the students for their achievement and revealed that the puzzles had been glued together and framed. She also informed readers that the puzzle works of art were so beautiful that the mayor decided to put them on display in the Oakville Public Library for all to admire.

Use the clues and the information in the introduction to figure out what was depicted in each puzzle work of art.

Clues

1. The number of pieces in each puzzle from youngest group to oldest group were 30, 50, 100, and 300. OPTIONAL: You may put these in the matrix grid if you wish.

2. The puzzle of the student whose name comes second alphabetically had twice as many pieces as the puzzle named "Playground Fun."

3. The puzzle that featured a lamb, a puppy, and a kitten had 20 pieces less than the puzzle that featured children playing in a playground.

4. The only puzzle with more pieces than Jimmy's was named "A Day at the Beach."

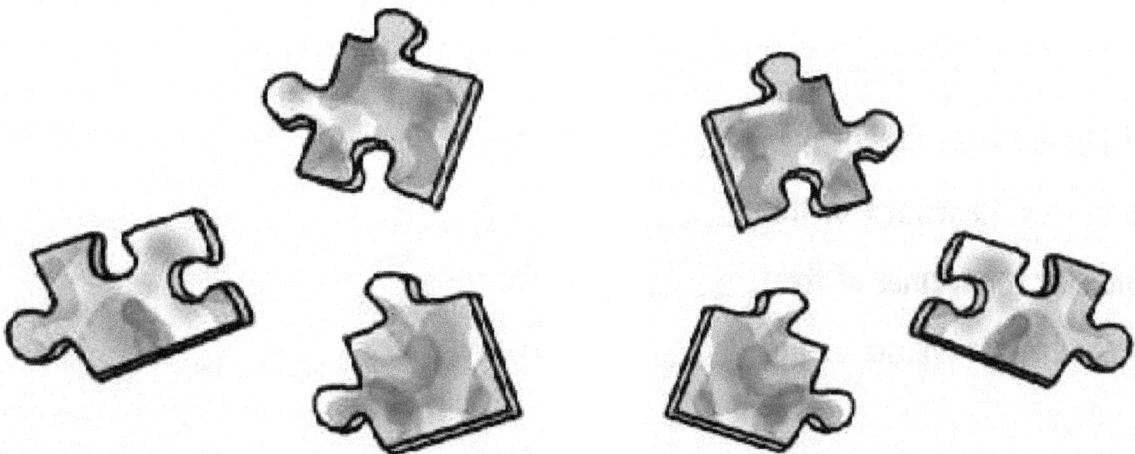

© Barbara M. Peller

Matrix for Works of Art!

	Playground Fun	Animal Babies	Jungle Scene	A Day at the Beach	30	50	100	300
Scarlet (K-2)								
Brianna (3-5)								
Jimmy (6-8)								
Rebecca (9-12)								

Scarlet's puzzle had ____ pieces and was named _____.

Brianna's puzzle had ____ pieces and was named _____.

Jimmy's puzzle had ____ pieces and was named _____.

Rebecca's puzzle had ____ pieces and was named _____.

Choose a Cupcake

Sara, Ella, Lily, and Isabella went to the Cupcake Bakery. There were so many choices that it was difficult for the girls to decide which to buy. Finally, they made their decisions! Three of the girls chose a chocolate cupcake; one chose a vanilla cupcake because she was allergic to chocolate. Each girl chose a different topping on vanilla icing. The toppings were cookie pieces, chocolate chips, rainbow sprinkles, and coconut flakes.

Use the clues and the information in the introduction to figure out what each chose.

Clues

1. Sara had the vanilla cupcake.

2. Sara was 8, Ella was 7, Lily was 9, and Isabella was 8.

3. The girl who chose the chocolate chips was neither the oldest nor the youngest.

4. The first girl to make her choice picked cookie pieces.

5. The girls chose their cupcakes in alphabetical order of their names.

6. It was hard to see the topping of the oldest girl's cupcake because it was white like the icing.

© **Barbara M. Peller**

Matrix for Choose a Cupcake

	Cookie Pieces	Chocolate Chips	Rainbow Sprinkles	Coconut Flakes
Sara				
Ella				
Lily				
Isabella				

Sara chose the _____.

Ella chose the _____.

Lily chose the _____.

Isabella chose the _____.

© Barbara M. Peller

A Day at the Circus

To celebrate Annie's birthday, Annie, her brother Bob, her mother, and her father went to the circus. The excitement began as soon as the ringmaster appeared in the center ring. The first act he announced was a pair of jugglers. The man and woman tossed multiple balls, hoops, bottles, bowling pins, and other items with amazing skill! The next act was a tightrope walker. Annie kept her eyes closed for the entire act, and she was very relieved when it was over and no harm had come to the performer. Other acts followed, and just before intermission a very small car appeared on the stage. The entire audience laughed as about twenty clowns emerged!

During intermission, Dad asked if anyone wanted a snack. Annie said she always wanted to try cotton candy, and Bob said he wanted a bag of peanuts. Mom asked for a box of popcorn. Dad went to the counter and bought the requested items for his family. He also bought a bottle of water for himself.

The highlight of the second half of the show was a team of acrobats from China. They performed breathtaking feats, such as forming towers by standing on one another's shoulders. In order to accomplish this, they were propelled into their position by jumping on a springboard. When a four-man-high tower was reached, the audience burst into applause! The show ended with a finale performed by the entire cast.

During the ride home, the family talked about their experience. Each favored a different act. Use the clues and the information in the story to figure out each person's favorite.

Clues

1. The family sat together in a row. (Hint: You might want to make a seating chart as you go along.)

2. The person who liked the clowns best sat between Annie and a stranger.

3. Bob sat next to the person whose favorite act involved people being propelled into the air.

4. The family member who did not have any food during intermission always sat on the aisle.

5. Mom could not stop laughing as the performers in her favorite act emerged from their vehicle.

6. Annie did not like the acrobats or the tightrope walker because she was afraid someone would fall.

   © **Barbara M. Peller**

Matrix for A Day at the Circus

	Clowns	Acrobats	Jugglers	Tightrope Walker
Annie				
Bob				
Mom				
Dad				

Annie liked the _____.

Bob liked the _____.

Mom liked the _____.

Dad liked the _____.

SEATING ARRANGEMENT:

© Barbara M. Peller

Vacation Fun

Hector, Oscar, Nicole, and Kimberly just got home from their family vacations. They all had a great time and were anxious to tell about their experiences. Each of the four friends described what they did: one went to the seashore, one went to a mountain resort, one went on a cruise, and one went to a theme park.

Use the clues and the information in the introduction to figure out where each friend went on vacation.

Clues:

1. The child who went to the seashore had never seen an ocean until then.

2. The girls whose name has three syllables is the youngest of the four friends.

3. Oscar told the person who went on the cruise that he took the same ocean cruise last year.

4. The friend who went to the theme park told Kimberly that he saw their math teacher there.

5. The girl who went to the seashore is older than the boy who went to the theme park.

6. The name of the girl who went on the cruise comes before the name of the boy who went to the mountains alphabetically.

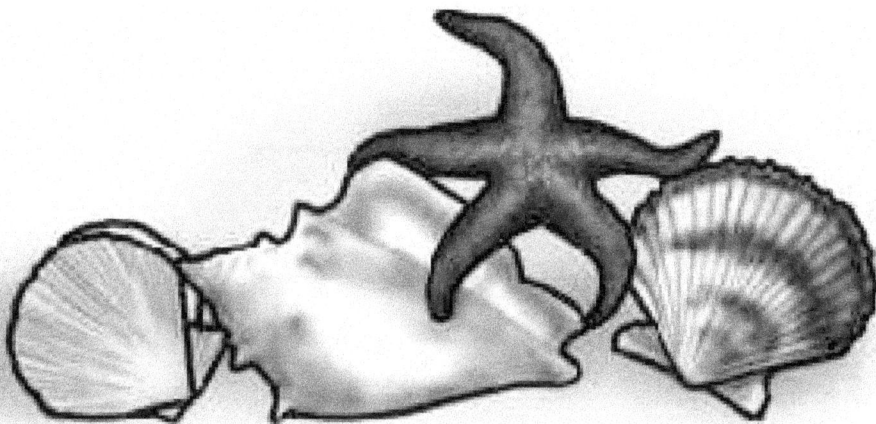

© **Barbara M. Peller**

Matrix for Vacation Fun

	Seashore	Mountain Resort	Cruise	Theme Park
Hector				
Oscar				
Nicole				
Kimberly				

Hector went _____.

Oscar went _____.

Nicole went _____.

Kimberly went _____.

© Barbara M. Peller

Who Won the Race?

The children in the fourth-grade class at Dogwood Elementary School were very excited. Every year the town held an End-of-the-Year Olympics. This year all four finalists in the 100-Meter Dash were from Dogwood Elementary: Elyssa, Ava, Ryan, and Jackson. Their last names were Gold, Silver, Thomas, and Leary.

Use the clues and the information in the introduction to figure out each child's last name. Then you will also know who won the race!

Clues

1. The last name of the boy whose first name comes third alphabetically is an anagram of a word that is an antonym of the word "late."

2. Ryan was faster than Jackson and the chid who's last name is Silver.

3. The child who's first name is a palindrome has a last name that is the name of a metal.

4. The girl who's last name is Gold lives next door to Elyssa.

5. Fill in the missing number in this pattern sequence to find out how many letters in the winner's first name.

1, 2, ___, 7, 11, 16, 22, 29

      © **Barbara M. Peller**

Matrix for Who Won the Race?

	Gold	Silver	Thomas	Leary
Elyssa				
Ava				
Ryan				
Jackson				

Elyssa _____

Ava _____

Ryan _____

Jackson _____

_____ ran the fastest.

© Barbara M. Peller

The Case of the Muddy Carpet

Mrs. French looked at her new carpet with pride. It was just installed the day before, and she really loved it. Imagine her dismay when she returned an hour later to find a trail of mud! The only possible culprits were Rocky, Samantha, Candy, and Tom. Their ages are 4, 8, 10, and 40.

Use the clues to figure out the ages of each of the suspects.

Clues:

1. The 40-year-old is Candy's father.

2. Candy is 6 years older than the one who muddied the carpet.

3. Rocky does not have any children.

4. The 8-year-old likes to take the one whose name has three vowels for a walk.

You should now know who muddied Mrs. French's carpet.

Complete this analogy to find out more about the one who muddied the carpet:

Feline : Cat :: Canine : _____

The one who muddied the carpet is a _____.

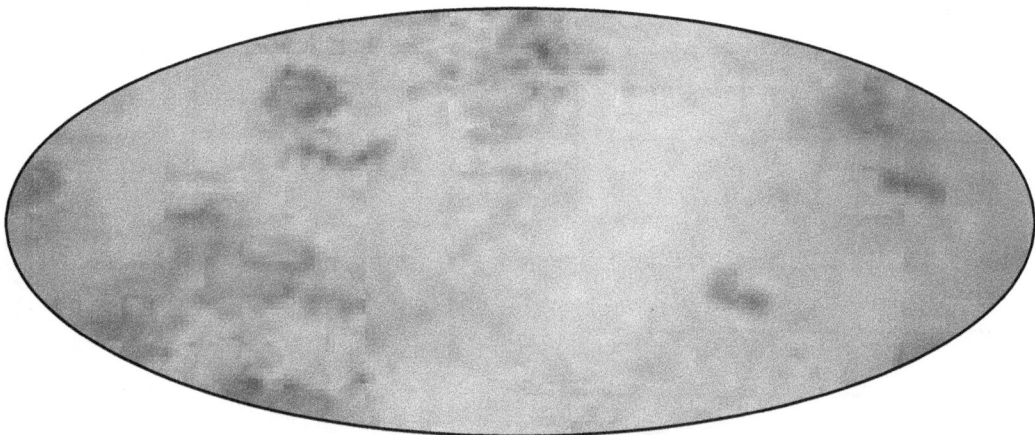

© Barbara M. Peller

Matrix for The Case of the Muddy Carpet

	4	8	10	40
Rocky				
Samantha				
Candy				
Tom				

Rocky is _____ years old.

Samantha is _____ years old.

Candy is _____ years old.

Tom is _____ years old.

_____ muddied the carpet!

The one who muddied the carpet is a _____.

© Barbara M. Peller

Level 2
Mysteries

© Barbara M. Peller

Precious Pet Parade

The town of Elmwood Ridge just held its annual Precious Pet Parade. Children from kindergarten through middle school were invited to march in the event. Some of the children marched with their animals alongside them on a leash while others carried their pets in a cage or in their arms. At the end of the parade, all the children were given certificates of participation, and a few prizes were awarded.

This year four friends aged six to nine— Lisa, Joey, Hunter, and Maria—entered their pets. The pets they entered were a dog, a bunny, a cat, and an iguana. The children and the animals all had a great time, and one of the animals was even awarded a prize for Most Unusual Pet.

Use the clues and the information given above to figure out the age of each child and which child entered each pet.

Clues:

1. Lisa was the oldest of the four friends.

2. The youngest brought the reptile.

3. Joey was a year older than Hunter and two years older than the child who brought a reptile.

4. Whoever brought the dog was three years older than the one who brought the reptile.

5. Solve the problem to find out the number of letters in the name of the boy who brought the bunny.

$$(28 \div 2 \div 14 + 25) - 22 = \rule{3cm}{0.4pt}$$

One of the pets won for Most Unusual Pet. Complete this syllogism to find out which:

A. A mammal did not win the prize for most unusual pet.

B. The bunny, the cat, and the dog are all mammals.

C. Therefore, _____.

Conclusion: _____.

© **Barbara M. Peller**

Matrix for Precious Pet Parade

	Dog	Bunny	Cat	Iguana	6	7	8	9
Lisa								
Joey								
Hunter								
Maria								

Lisa is ____ and entered a _____.

Joey is ____ and entered a _____.

Hunter is ____ and entered a _____.

Maria is ____ and entered a _____.

_____ won the prize for Most Unusual Pet.

The Case of the Melted Ice Cream

Liz and her friends Kate, Matt, and Jeff went to Liz's house after school to work on a school project. Before they began their work, Liz asked her mother if they could have a snack. Her mom said, "Sure, as long as you clean up and put everything away before you leave the kitchen. I am expecting company, so I want the house to be clean and neat!" The children all agreed, and Mom left the room. As soon as she left, the children each chose a different snack. One had a peanut butter and jelly sandwich, one had some freshly baked cookies, one had an apple, and one had a bowl of ice cream.

A few hours later Liz's mother came into the kitchen to begin to prepare dinner. On the counter she saw an almost-full container of completely melted ice cream! One of the children did not clean up as promised!

Use the clues and the information in the introduction to figure out which child had each snack and who left the ice cream on the counter.

Clues:

1. Two of the four children are cousins. None of the others are related.

2. The boy who ate the fruit is older than the girl who ate the ice cream.

3. The same child who ate the ice cream was responsible for leaving it on the counter.

4. Jeff, the oldest child, asked the girl who ate the cookies if he could taste a small piece.

5. The name of the girl who ate the cookies is an anagram of a word meaning "to reach for and hold."

6. The child who ate the peanut butter and jelly sandwich and the child who ate the ice cream are cousins.

7. Jeff's father and Liz's mother are brother and sister.

Logic Mysteries for Young Readers   © Barbara M. Peller

Matrix for The Case of the Melted Ice Cream

	P, B, & J Sandwich	Cookies	Apple	Ice Cream
Liz				
Kate				
Matt				
Jeff				

Liz had _____.

Kate had _____.

Matt had _____.

Jake had _____.

_____ left the ice cream on the counter.

Who Opened Tweety's Cage?

Someone let Tweety, the Conners' pet bird, out of his cage. It took Mrs. Conner thirty minutes to get Tweety back into the cage, which was hanging from a wall in the kitchen. Mrs. Conner had four suspects: Sammy, Liam, Tom, and Danny. She knew that each one was in a different room at the time the cage was left open, but she did not know who was in each room. If she could figure out who was in the kitchen, she would know who opened the cage.

Use the clues and the information in the introduction to figure out where each was when the cage was opened and who left the cage open.

Clues:

1. The bedroom was the only room in the house with a view of the hammock.

2. The boy whose name is an anagram of a word that means "letters and packages delivered by the postal system" had not been outside all day because of his allergies.

3. Danny liked to play ball with Tom and the boy in the bedroom.

4. Sammy and Danny were on the same soccer team as the boy in the dining room.

5. When Sammy looked through the window, he could see Danny reading a book in the hammock.

6. Danny said good-bye to Liam as he passed the dining room on his way out of the house.

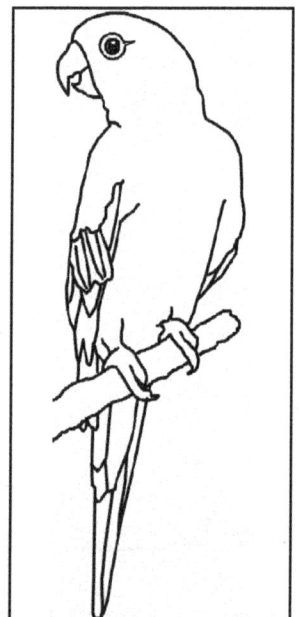

Change one letter at a time to find out more about Tom:

TOM

_____ a young child

_____ a type of bed

_____ a small mammal with soft fur and a short snout

Tom is a _____.

    © **Barbara M. Peller**

Matrix for Who Opened Tweety's Cage?

	Kitchen	Bedroom	Dining Room	Backyard
Sammy				
Liam				
Tom				
Danny				

Sammy was in the _____.

Liam was in the _____.

Tom was in the _____.

Danny was in the _____.

_____ left the cage door open.

TOM ⚬○_____ ⚬○_____ ⚬○_____   Tom is a _____.

© Barbara M. Peller   *Logic Mysteries for Young Readers*

The Case of the Potted Plant

Mrs. Penny Potter was very proud of her potted plant. She even planned to enter it in the contest held at the Pottsville Plant Festival. The festival would take place in the park. The night before the festival, Mrs. Potter went into the living room to take a peek at her plant. As she entered the room, she pictured herself being presented with a prize. Imagine her disappointment when she saw that her perfect plant was lying on the floor! Mrs. Potter was sure that one of her pets was responsible. They included a dog, a cat, a guinea pig, and a parrot. Their names were Max, Penny, Spot, and Tigger.

Use the clues to figure out what type of animal each pet was and which one knocked over the potted plant.

Clues

1. Tigger is larger than Spot but smaller than the dalmatian.

2. The rodent is smaller than Tigger.

3. The bird is not named after a character in *Winnie the Pooh*.

4. Penny is the only animal that is not a mammal.

Fill in the blank to complete the analogy. Then use the solution to fill in the blank in the sentence to figure out which pet knocked over the plant

fish : fins :: _____ : feathers

A _____ knocked over the plant!

Extra: What form of figurative language was used in the story? Use that form of figurative language to tell who knocked over the plant.

_____

_____

© **Barbara M. Peller**

Matrix for The Case of the Potted Plant

	Dog	Cat	Guinea Pig	Parrot
Max				
Penny				
Spot				
Tigger				

Max is a _____.

Penny is a _____.

Spot is a _____.

Tigger is a _____.

_____ knocked over the plant.

_____ was the type of figurative language used.

© Barbara M. Peller

Who Wrote the Note?

Jessica came home and found a note taped to her front door. It read, "I want to show you something. Meet me at my house this afternoon at 5:00 p.m." The note was signed "Your friend, Jane." Jessica has four friends named Jane. Their last names are Canby, Jordan, Brook, and Lewis. Two (and only two) of the girls are related. The streets the girls live on are Main, Central, First, and Lincoln.

Use the clues to find out which girl lives on each street and which girl wrote the note.

Clues

1. Jane Brook and the girl who lives on First Street are cousins.

2. Jane Lewis is the oldest of the five girls.

3. Jane Jordan lives two blocks from the girl who lives on First Street and four blocks from the girl who lives on Lincoln Street.

4. Jane Jordan is older than the girl who lives on Main Street.

5. The name of the girl who lives on Lincoln Street comes after the name of the girl who lives on First Street alphabetically.

6. The girl who wrote the note asked Jane Canby, her cousin, to go with her to tape the note to Jessica's door.

Change one letter at a time to find out what Jane wanted to show Jessica:

NOTE

_____ a nickname for Nathan

_____ opposite of early

_____ a body of water

_____ to cook with dry heat

_____ a vehicle with 2 wheels

Jane wanted to show her a _____.

> Dear Jessica,
> I want to show you something. Meet me at my house this afternoon at 5:00 p.m.
> Your friend,
> Jane

© Barbara M. Peller

Matrix for Who Wrote the Note?

	Main	Central	First	Lincoln
Canby				
Jordan				
Brook				
Lewis				

Jane Canby lived on _____.

Jane Jordan lived on _____.

Jane Brook lived on _____.

Jane Lewis lived on _____.

_____ wrote the note.

NOTE ◦◦ _____ ◦◦ _____ ◦◦ _____ ◦◦ _____ ◦◦ _____

She wanted to show Jessica a _____.

Working for a Good Cause

The annual Willow Grove Carnival was held at the town's recreation complex. The local boy-scout troop set up three booths to raise money. From one booth they sold shirts, from another they sold raffle tickets, and from another they sold different types of food. The money they raised would be donated to the New Playground Fund.

Four friends—Jim, Jake, Jamal, and Josh—were the first to volunteer to help at the carnival. One signed up to sell Italian ices at the food booth, one volunteered to sell shirts with the town name, and one said he would sell raffle tickets. The fourth signed up to help clean up after the fair was over.

The event was very successful, and the scouts' booths did especially well! They were able to donate even more money than they had hoped. At the end of the event, the winning raffle number was called. One of the four friends won the big prize—a new video-game system!

Use these clues to figure out which friend was on each committee and who won the prize.

Clues

1. The child who cleaned up takes guitar lessons with the child who sold food.

2. Jim never had any type of music lesson.

3. The tallest child sold raffle tickets.

4. Jim is shorter than Jamal and taller than the others.

5. The boy whose name is also a verb meaning "to tease in a playful way" bought ices from the child who sold food.

6. The name of the child who won the raffle comes third alphabetically.

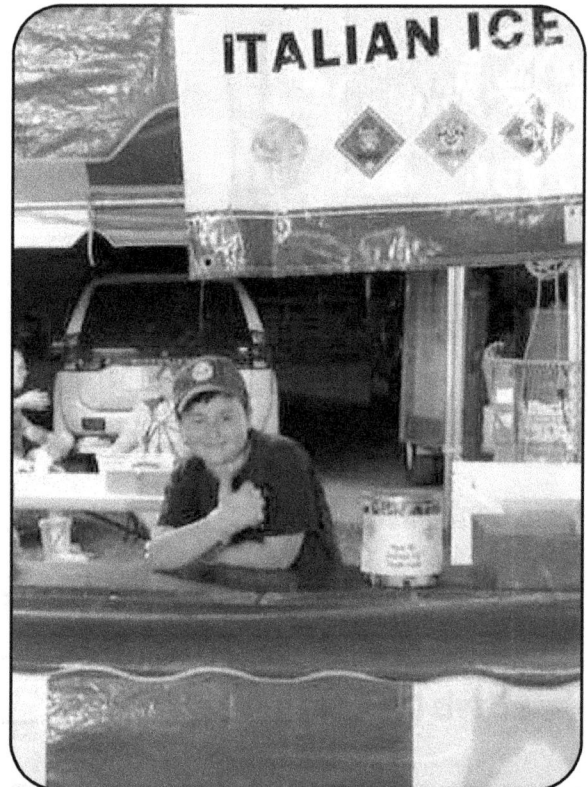

© **Barbara M. Peller**

Matrix for Working for a Good Cause

	Food	Tickets	Shirts	Clean-up
Jim				
Jake				
Jamal				
Josh				

Jim was on the _____ Committee.

Jake was on the _____ Committee.

Jamal was on the _____ Committee.

Josh was on the _____ Committee.

_____ won the prize.

© Barbara M. Peller

A Trip to the Zoo

Mrs. Nixon's first-grade class went on a field trip to the zoo. For homework, the children were asked to draw their favorite zoo animal. Amanda, Nick, April, and Ashley forgot to put their names on their drawings. The animals they drew were giraffe, elephant, lamb, and tiger.

Use the clues to help Mrs. Nixon figure out who drew each animal.

Clues

1. A girl's favorite animal had a trunk.

2. The oldest child chose an animal that was in the petting zoo.

3. The youngest child chose the tiger.

4. The only one whose name does not start with a vowel and Amanda are twins. They are five months older than the youngest child and one week younger than the oldest child.

5. Because their birthdays are so close together, Amanda and the girl whose name is a month of the year sometimes celebrate together.

None of these animals was the most popular. Unscramble the letters to find out which animal was drawn by the most students.

OMNEYK

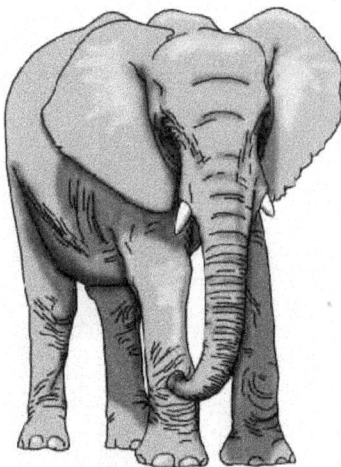

© **Barbara M. Peller**

Matrix for A Trip to the Zoo

	Giraffe	Elephant	Lamb	Tiger
Amanda				
Nick				
April				
Ashley				

Amanda drew _____.

Nick drew _____.

April drew _____.

Ashley drew _____.

The _____ was the most popular choice.

© Barbara M. Peller

Who Took Grandma's Laptop?

Grandma Ruth loved her new laptop. She was always busy searching the web, sending emails, and reading her friends' posts on the social network. Imagine her surprise when she went to get it from the kitchen table and found that is was not there! She was using it only a few minutes ago, and only four people were in the house with her: Rachel, Lauren, Olivia, and Sophia. One was her sister, one was her daughter, one was her ten-year-old granddaughter, and one was her granddaughter's friend from her class. The friend was not related to any of the others.

Use the clues to find out their relationships.

Clues

1. Sophia did not meet Ruth's granddaughter's friend until that day.

2. Lauren is 6 months younger than Ruth's granddaughter.

3. Lauren and Sophia were playing checkers at the kitchen table when Ruth entered the room.

4. Rachel was watching television in the living room while Ruth searched for her laptop.

5. Ruth's granddaughter and Rachel both refer to Sophia as Aunt Sophie.

6. The person who took the laptop was using it in the dining room.

Now that you know the relationships, reread the clues to determine which one took the computer.

© Barbara M. Peller

Matrix for Who Took Grandma's Laptop?

	Sister	Daughter	Granddaughter	Friend of Granddaughter
Rachel				
Lauren				
Olivia				
Sophia				

Rachel was _____.

Lauren was _____.

Olivia was _____.

Sophia was _____.

_____ took the laptop.

Who Rang the Doorbell?

Jason was watching TV one Saturday morning when the doorbell rang. When he went to the door, no one was there. As soon as he sat down, the doorbell rang again. Jason was sure that one of his four best friends was playing a trick on him. He called each boy and asked where he was. His friends were named Cole, Mario, Nathan, and Cameron. These are the places they said they were: the library, the supermarket, the zoo, and the new bookstore in town. One of the boys was lying.

Use these clues to figure out where each boy said that he was when Jason called.

Clues

1. The boys ages are 9, 9, 10, and 12.

2. The boy who said he was in the bookstore is two years older than Cameron and three years older than the twins.

3. Mario has no siblings.

4. Neither twin said he was at the supermarket.

5. The boy whose name is a homonym for a word that means "a type of substance used as fuel" said he was at the zoo.

One of the boys was not where he said he was! He was really at Jason's house ringing the bell! Solve the problem to figure out who was lying!

These are the boys ages:

Cameron: _____

Mario: _____

Cole: _____

Nathan: _____

The age of the boy who rang the bell was the average age of the boys.

© **Barbara M. Peller**

Matrix for Who Rang the Doorbell?

	Library	Supermarket	Zoo	bookstore
Cole				
Mario				
Nathan				
Cameron				

Cole said he was at the _____.

Mario said he was at the _____.

Nathan said he was at the _____.

Cameron said he was at the _____.

The average age of the boys was _____.

_____ rang the bell.

The Case of the Broken Vase

When Mom and Dad came home from an evening at the theater, they noticed that the floor was wet. Then they saw that a broken vase and the flowers that had been in it were lying on the floor. The babysitter and the three children were each in a different place. The names of the babysitter and the three children were Samantha, Tyler, Rick, and Angie. One was in the kitchen, one was in the living room, one was in the library, and one was on the deck.

Use the clues to figure out who was in each place.

Clues

1. The babysitter was in charge of the three children.

2. Before Mom and Dad left, they asked the babysitter to make sure that Angie finished her homework.

3. The babysitter was in the library when she heard the vase fall.

4. Rick asked his sister, who was watching a movie in the living room, to turn down the television set.

5. Tyler had asked Rick to join him on the deck, but Rick said he had to do his homework.

Who knocked over the vase? Put a check next to the information you still need to solve this mystery.

___ The age of the babysitter.
___ The age of the children.
___ The location of the vase when it was knocked down.
___ The kind of flowers that were in the vase.

Challenge Activity:
Solve this coded message to figure out where the vase was!
HINT: SGD = THE

SGD UZRD VZR HM SGD JHSBGDM.

© **Barbara M. Peller**

Matrix for The Case of the Broken Vase

	Kitchen	Living Room	Library	Deck
Samantha				
Tyler				
Rick				
Angie				

Samantha was _____.

Tyler was _____.

Rick was _____.

Angie was _____.

MESSAGE: _____.

_____ knocked over the vase.

© Barbara M. Peller

Level 3 Mysteries

© Barbara M. Peller

The Case of the Missing Pie

Mom wasn't hungry when dessert was served, so she decided to save her piece of pie for the next day. She asked everyone to please save the pie for her. However, the next afternoon when she went to the refrigerator to get her piece of pie, all she found was the plate and a few crumbs. The only ones in the house besides her were her husband (referred to as Dad), her two children, and her children's two friends. Their names in alphabetical order were Brooke, Ellie, Logan, Mike, and Samuel. Their ages were 14, 15, 16, 17, and 45.

Clues

1. Her daughter's friend is a girl and her son's friend is a boy.

2. The sum of the ages of the three youngest is equal to the age of Dad.

3. The sum of Brooke's and her friend's ages is 33.

4. Dad is three times as old as Mike.

5. Neither Mike nor Ellie has siblings.

6. Logan is 2 years younger than his sister and 31 years younger than his father.

Reread the clues to determine the relationships of each.

Solve this problem to find out the age of the person who ate Mom's pie:

$$4 (6 + 2) - 18 = \underline{\hspace{3in}}$$

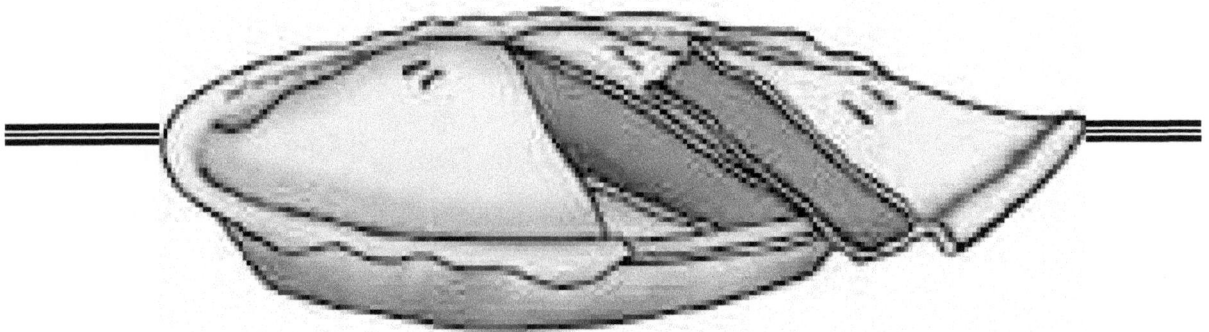

                                        © **Barbara M. Peller**

Matrix for The Case of the Missing Pie

	14	15	16	17	45	Husband	Daughter	Son	Friend of Daughter	Friend of Son
Samuel										
Brooke										
Ellie										
Logan										
Mike										

Samuel was _____ years old.   Relationship to Mom: _____

Brooke was _____ years old.   Relationship to Mom: _____

Ellie was _____ years old.   Relationship to Mom: _____

Logan was _____ years old.   Relationship to Mom: _____

Mike was _____ years old.   Relationship to Mom: _____

_____ ate Mom's pie.

The Case of the Missing Library Book

Mrs. Jones, the town librarian, noticed that a newly arrived book was missing from the shelves of the Oakville Public Library. She was especially upset because the book was written by a best-selling author who lived in Oakville. The title of the book was *Mystery on Oakwood Drive*. Mrs. Jones had five suspects: Mr. Green, Miss Nicely, Miss January, Miss Saturn, and Mr. Write. Their occupations were police officer, dentist, author, banker, and teacher. Each of them had been in the library when the book arrived.

Clues

1. Mr. Green lives next door to the police officer.

2. Both the person whose name is a verb and the person whose name is an adverb are patients of the dentist.

3. The teacher is a patient of the person whose name is a planet in our solar system.

4. Mr. Green and Miss January live in opposite sides of the town.

5. The author, the police officer and the person whose name is a verb went to the same high school.

6. Mr. Write's daughter is a student in Mr. Green's class.

Challenge Activity:

Solve this coded message to figure out who took the book and why!
HINT: CPPL = BOOK

UIF BVUIPS UPPL UIF

CPPL UP TJHO JU!

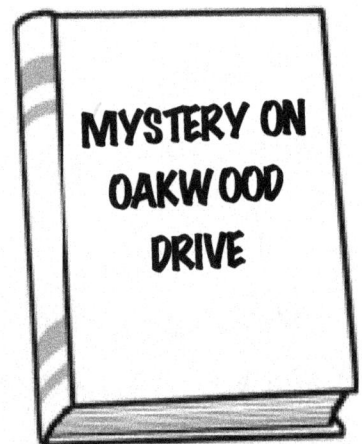

© **Barbara M. Peller**

Matrix for The Case of the Missing Library Book

	Police Officer	Dentist	Author	Banker	Teacher
Mr. Green					
Miss Nicely					
Miss January					
Miss Saturn					
Mr. Write					

Mr. Green is _____.

Miss Nicely is _____.

Miss January is _____.

Miss Saturn is _____.

Mr. Write is _____.

MESSAGE: _____.

_____ took the book.

Who Woke Grandpa?

Grandpa was sound asleep. Suddenly he awoke. Someone had tickled his foot with a feather! He was sure it was one of his grandchildren, but which one? Grandpa had four grandchildren: 2 boys and 2 girls, each with a different color hair. None of the children admitted tickling his foot! Alanna said she thought it was Dylan. Dylan said he thought it was Megan. Megan said it was probably Aidan. Aidan said he didn't have any idea who did it.

Use these clues to figure out which grandchild was in Grandpa's bedroom. That will also be the one who tickled his foot! HINT: You will have to keep track of the color of each child's hair!

Clues

1. Both girls saw the blond go into the dining room.

2. The redhead peeked around the kitchen door when she heard Grandpa laugh.

3. Alanna envied her sister's red hair.

4. Neither Alanna nor Dylan has black hair.

5. One of the girls was playing a guitar in the living room when Grandpa was tickled.

© **Barbara M. Peller**

Matrix for Who Woke Grandpa?

	Kitchen	Living Room	Dining Room	Bedroom	Brown	Black	Blond	Red
Alanna								
Dylan								
Megan								
Aidan								

Alanna was in the _____. She had _____ hair.

Dylan was in the _____. He had _____ hair.

Megan was in the _____. She had _____ hair.

Aidan was in the _____. He had _____ hair.

_____ woke Grandpa.

© Barbara M. Peller

A Group Project

Oliver, Ruth, Sadie, Jackson, and Meg were working together on a group project for their social studies class. They made a list of materials they needed to complete the project. On the list were these items: colored pencils, poster board, paint, colored paper, glue, and a pair of scissors. As there were six items and only five people, one child agreed to get two of the items. The other four would each get one item. They all agreed to bring the items to their next meeting.

Clues

1. The girl who got the paint did not get any other item.

2. The boy who got the colored paper is Meg's cousin.

3. The child who got the poster board lives two blocks from Jackson and four blocks from the boy who got the colored pencils.

4. One of the girls got 2 items.

5. Ruth and the person who got the glue are best friends.

6. The girl whose name is an anagram of a word that means "a precious or semiprecious stone" rides the school bus each day with the girls who got the poster board and the paint.

7. The name of the girl who got two items comes second alphabetically.

8. Ruth and the girl who got poster board went to the store together to buy the items.

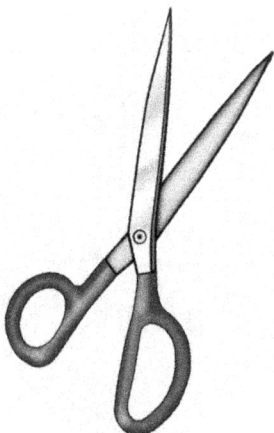

© **Barbara M. Peller**

Matrix for A Group Project

	Colored Pencils	Poster Board	Paint	Colored Paper	Glue	Scissors
Oliver						
Ruth						
Sadie						
Jackson						
Meg						

Oliver agreed to get the _____.

Ruth agreed to get the _____.

Sadie agreed to get the _____.

Jackson agreed to get the _____.

Meg agreed to get the _____.

© Barbara M. Peller

A Costume Contest

The Maple Grove Costume Contest was held every year at Maple Grove Recreation Center. This year the four winners were Karl, Carlos, Abigail, and Alyssa. One was dressed as an astronaut, one was a storybook character, one was a robot, and one was a unicorn. They won prizes in these categories: Cutest, Most Original, Most Accurate, and Funniest.

Use the clues to figure out who wore each costume and the prize won by each.

Clues

1. The one who dressed like a robot took the school bus every day.

2. Alyssa and the unicorn were on the same soccer team.

3. The unicorn and the boy who won for Funniest Costume were cousins.

4. Carlos admired the costume of the boy dressed as a President.

5. The girl who won for Most Original Costume was wearing a space suit.

6. The contestant who won for the Most Accurate Costume was wearing a top hat.

7. The one who won for Most Original Costume walked to school every day with Abigail and the boy whose name is an anagram for a type of songbird.

© **Barbara M. Peller**

Matrix for A Costume Contest

	Astronaut	Abraham Lincoln	Robot	Unicorn	Cutest	Original	Accurate	Funniest
Karl								
Carlos								
Abigail								
Alyssa								

Carl was dressed as _____ and won _____.

Carlos was dressed as _____ and won _____.

Abigail was dressed as _____ and won _____.

Alyssa was dressed as _____ and won _____.

Who Played What?

Lacy, Heather, Frank, Summer, and Conner are all members of the Elmwood Park Elementary School orchestra. They played the following instruments: violin, cello, trumpet, flute, and drums. Tonight was the Spring Concert, and all of the children are very excited. They have practiced for weeks and feel very prepared. Two of the children will even be performing a solo.

HELPFUL INFORMATION

1. The flute is a woodwind instrument.
2. The trumpet is a brass instrument.
3. The violin and cello are string instruments.
4. Drums are percussion instruments.

Use the clues and the above information to figure out who played each instrument.

Clues

1. Only one student's name and instrument begin with the same letter.

2. The children are all in the fourth or fifth grade. Only fifth graders are given solos.

3. Heather lives on the same block as the fifth-grade student who plays the percussion instrument.

4. The name of the violinist is one of the four seasons.

5. The violinist got a standing ovation after her performance.

6. The one whose name comes first alphabetically plays the instrument whose name comes first alphabetically.

7. Three of the children are in the fourth grade.

8. The child whose name is an anagram for a word that means "a type of material often used in pottery" walks to school with the girl who plays the flute.

9. Frank is in the fourth grade.

Reread the clues to figure out which two students had the solos.

© Barbara M. Peller

Matrix for Who Played What?

	Violin	Cello	Trumpet	Flute	Drums
Lacy					
Heather					
Frank					
Summer					
Conner					

Lacy played the _____.

Heather played the _____.

Frank played the _____.

Summer played the _____.

Conner played the _____.

_____ and _____ had solos.

© Barbara M. Peller

The Case of the Open Door

When Mr. Costa came downstairs, he noticed that there were several flies in the house and that the front door was wide open. "Who left the door open and let all these flies in the house?" Mr. Costa asked, sounding very annoyed. In the house with Mr. Costa were his wife, his mother, his aunt, his daughter, and his niece. Their names were Anna, Barbara, Melissa, Sofia, and Taylor; their ages were 12, 15, 34, 36, and 70.

Use the clues and the above information to figure out the age of each person and her relationship to Mr. Costa.

Clues

1. The sum of the ages of Mr. Costa's wife and sister equals the age of his mother.

2. Barbara is three years older than Mr. Costa's daughter.

3. The 70-year-old and Taylor just came back from shopping.

4. Mr. Costa and his sister are twins.

5. The person whose name is a homonym of a word that means "a person who makes or repairs garments" did not leave the door open.

6. Melissa is three years younger than her cousin Barbara.

7. The name of Mr. Costa's wife is a palindrome.

8. Mr. Costa's wife is two years younger than his sister.

Figure out the perimeter of this rectangle to find out the age of the person who left the door open!

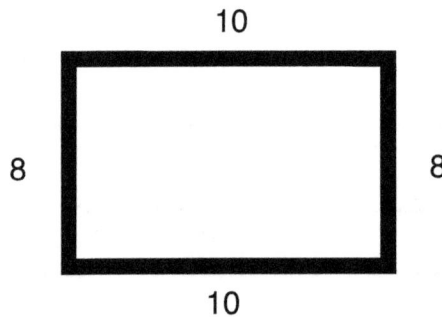

10

8   8

10

Who left the door open? How do we know?

_____

_____

                    © **Barbara M. Peller**

Matrix for The Case of the Open Door

	Wife	Mother	Sister	Daughter	Niece	12	15	36	34	70
Anna										
Barbara										
Melissa										
Sofia										
Taylor										

Anna is Mr. Costa's _____ and is _____ years old.

Barbara is Mr. Costa's _____ and is _____ years old.

Melissa is Mr. Costa's _____ and is _____ years old.

Sofia is Mr. Costa's _____ and is _____ years old.

Taylor is Mr. Costa's _____ and is _____ years old.

The person who left the door open is _____ years old.

_____ left the door open!

The Case of the Missing Project

The fourth graders of Pine Grove Elementary School just completed a unit on famous people. Each child chose a famous man or woman and did a special project that tells something about that person's achievements. Their teacher told them that their projects would be put on display in the hallway for Back-to-School Night.

Before they left for home on the afternoon of Back-to-School Night Neil, Isabella, Eric, Becca, and Emily looked for their projects in the hallway. The people they had chosen were George Washington, Abraham Lincoln, Dr. Seuss, Thomas Edison, and Sacajawea. The projects were a painting, a poster, a written report, a poem, and a song. Four of the children found their projects; however, one of the projects was missing! It was not in the hallway!

Use the clues and the information in the story to figure out which famous person each child chose, the type of project each did, whose project was missing, and where the missing project was.

Clues

1. The person who wrote the poem about an author is in Isabella's reading group.

2. Emily is older than Becca and younger than the boy who chose an inventor.

3. A girl wrote a song about a President.

4. Becca admired her friend's painting of George Washington.

5. The person whose name comes first alphabetically wrote the report.

6. Emily's project was entitled "Our Sixteenth President."

7. Becca wrote about the woman who helped Lewis and Clark during their famous expedition.

8. The student whose name is an anagram of the name of a common food item used pictures of a light bulb and a phonograph in the creation of his project.

9. The poem was not in the hallway.

Complete this analogy to get a clue about where the missing project was.

Paintings : Art Gallery :: Books : _____

The project is on display in the _____.

                          © Barbara M. Peller

The Case of the Missing Project

	George Washington	Abraham Lincoln	Dr. Seuss	Thomas Edison	Sacajawea	Painting	Poster	Report	Poem	Song
Neil										
Isabella										
Eric										
Becca										
Emily										

Neil's project was a _____ about _____.

Isabella's project was a _____ about _____.

Eric's project was a _____ about _____.

Becca's project was a _____ about _____.

Emily's project was a _____ about _____.

_____'s project was missing.

It was _____.

© Barbara M. Peller

Celebrating America Song Festival

The teachers of Woodland Park Elementary School were extremely proud of their students. They had just performed at the annual Celebrating America Song Festival and all did a fantastic job. The names of the teachers are Mrs. Arms, Mrs. Cape, Miss Green, Mr. Allan, and Mr. Ray. Each class sang a different song. The songs they performed were "The Star-Spangled Banner," "Yankee Doodle Dandy," "You're a Grand Old Flag," "America the Beautiful," and "This Land Is Your Land."

Use the clues and the story information to figure out who taught each grade and what song each grade sang.

Clues

1. Mr. Allan was new to the school and had never before attended the festival.

2. Woodland Park Elementary is a K through 5 school, but only grades 1 to 5 perform.

3. Only students in grades 4 or 5 had a solo.

4. The last name of the teacher of the oldest students is also a man's first name.

5. The teacher whose name comes first alphabetically teaches the youngest students.

6. The class that sang "Yankee Doodle Dandy" was performing for the first time.

7. The class that sang "The Star-Spangled Banner" sang the same song at the festival two years ago.

8. The name of the third-grade teacher is also the name of an article of clothing.

9. A student whose class sang "America the Beautiful" also had a solo.

10. Mr. Ray's class sang "This Land Is Your Land."

11. The teacher whose name is a color car pools with the teacher whose class sang "You're a Grand Old Flag."

Challenge Activity:

Do you notice anything unusual about the teachers when listed from grade 1 to grade 5? Solve this coded message to find out what it is! HINT: BSF = ARE

UIF OBNFT BSF JO BMQIBCFUJDBM PSEFS.

© Barbara M. Peller

Matrix for Celebrating America Song Festival

	Mrs. Arms	Mrs. Cape	Miss Green	Mr. Allan	Mr. Ray	Star-Spangled Banner	Yankee Doodle Dandy	You're a Grand Old Flag	America the Beautiful	This Land Is Your Land
Grade 1										
Grade 2										
Grade 3										
Grade 4										
Grade 5										

Grade 1 Teacher: _____ Song: _____

Grade 2 Teacher: _____ Song: _____

Grade 3 Teacher: _____ Song: _____

Grade 4 Teacher: _____ Song: _____

Grade 5 Teacher: _____ Song: _____

Message: _____

_____.

Pen Pals

As part of their unit on letter writing, Mrs. Kennedy decided to have the children in her fifth-grade class write to pen pals in other states. She obtained a list of names and addresses of children who were looking for pen pals. Then Mrs. Kennedy wrote each name and address on a slip of paper and put the slips into a box. Each child took a turn reaching into the box and picking a name.

Within two weeks, all of the children had received mail back from their pen pals. Five friends—Juan, Elle, Hannah, Otto, and Charlotte—met one day after school and talked about their new pen pals. The names of their pen pals were Madison, Austin, Savannah, Gary, and May. The states they lived in were California, Georgia, North Carolina, Texas, and Wisconsin.

Use the clues and information in the story to figure out the name of each friend's pen pal and the state in which the pen pal lived.

Clues

1. Two of the pen pals have a name that is also the name of a city in the state in which he or she lives.

2. Charlotte thought it was funny that her name was the same as the name of the city in which her pen pal lived. In fact, her pen pal told her that it was the largest city in the state.

3. The name of the girl whose pen pal was named Madison is a palindrome.

4. Savannah does not live in Georgia.

5. The girl whose name comes first alphabetically has a pen pal in Georgia.

6. The name of Charlotte's pen pal is the name of a city in the state where Hannah's pen pal lives.

7. Otto's pen pal lives in Houston.

8. The name of the girl whose name is a month has never been to California.

© Barbara M. Peller

Matrix for Pen Pals

	CA	GA	NC	TX	WI	Madison	Austin	Savannah	Gary	May
Juan										
Elle										
Hannah										
Otto										
Charlotte										
	CA	GA	NC	TX	WI	Juan	Elle	Hannah	Otto	Charlotte
Madison										
Austin										
Savannah										
Gary										
May										

Juan's pen pal is named _____ and lives in _____.

Elle's pen pal is named _____ and lives in _____.

Ava's pen pal is named _____ and lives in _____.

Otto's pen pal is named _____ and lives in _____.

Charlotte's pen pal is named _____ and lives in _____.

© Barbara M. Peller

Title: _____   **By:** _____

Story:

_____

_____

_____

_____

_____

_____

_____

_____

_____

_____

_____

_____

Clues

1. _____

2. _____

3. _____

4. _____

5. _____

6. _____

7. _____

8. _____

9. _____

10. _____

© **Barbara M. Peller**

Matrix for _____?

_____

_____

_____

_____

_____

_____

© Barbara M. Peller

• • • • Explanations of the Solutions • • • •

LEVEL 1 MYSTERIES

Scoops for You
Clue No. 1 and the information in the story tell us that Jennie did not have 2 scoops, 3 scoops, or the sundae; therefore, she ordered 1 scoop.
Clue No. 2 tells us Eli did not have 3 scoops.
Clue No. 3 tells us Carolina had the sundae. We now Becca had 3 scoops and Eli had 2 scoops.

Which Sport?
Clue No. 1 tells us Austin did not play field hockey.
Clue No. 2 tells us that Ethan favors baseball.
Clue No. 3 tells us Jacob doesn't favor soccer or field hockey. We now know that Jacob favors basketball. We also know that Andrew favors field hockey and Austin favors soccer.

A Foul-Shooting Competition
Clue No. 1 tells us that Justin is not named Apple. We also know Rebecca is not named Apple and Justin made 17 shots.
Clue No. 3 tells us Zack's name is Black and he made 20 shots. We now know Brad's name is Apple. With **Clues No. 1 and 2** we know Brad made 19 shots. We also know Rebecca made 23 and won the contest.
Clue No. 4 tells us Rebecca is named Green and Justin is named Rose.

The Oakville Town Fair Puzzle Contest
Clue No. 3 tells us that Jimmy was not in the Grades K–2 Group.
Clue No. 4 and **Clue No. 2** tell us that Brianna was not in the oldest or youngest group.
Clue No. 5 tells us that Scarlet was the winner of the Grades K–2 Group. We now also know that Rebecca was the winner of the Grades 9–12 Group.
Clue No. 6 and **Clue No. 1** tell us that Jimmy won in the Grades 6–8 Group. We now also know that Brianna won in the Grades 3–5 Group.

Works of Art
Clue No. 1 tells us the number of pieces in each.
Clue No. 2 and **Clue No. 1** tell us "Playground Fun" had 50 pieces and was, therefore, Brianna's puzzle.
Clue No. 3 and **Clue No. 2** tell us that Scarlet's puzzle was named "Animal Babies."
Clue No. 4 tells us Jimmy's puzzle was named "Jungle Scene" and Rebecca's puzzle was "A Day at the Beach."

Choose a Cupcake
Clue No. 1 and the story tell us that Sara did not have chocolate chips.
Clue No. 3 and **Clue No. 2** tell us that neither Lily nor Ella had chocolate chips. We now know that Isabella had chocolate chips.
Clue No. 5 and **Clue No. 4** tell us Ella had cookie pieces.
Clue No. 6 and **Clue No. 2** tell us that Lily chose coconut flakes. We now also know that Sara chose rainbow sprinkles.

A Day at the Circus
Clue No. 1 tells us they sat together in a row.
Clue No. 2 tells us that Annie did not prefer the clowns and that whoever did sat at one end.
Clue No. 3 tells us Bob did not like the acrobats best.
Clue No. 4 and information in the story tell us Dad was on the aisle at the other end. With **Clue No. 2** we know he did not prefer the clowns. We now also know Bob sat between Annie and Dad. With **Clue No. 3** we know that either Dad or Annie preferred the acrobats.
Clue No. 5 tells us Mom liked the clowns best.
Clue No. 6 tells us Annie didn't like the acrobats or the tightrope walker; therefore, she liked the jugglers. We now know Dad liked the acrobats and Bob liked the tightrope walker.
SEATING: STRANGER Mom Annie Bob Dad AISLE

Vacation Fun
Clue No. 3 tells us that Oscar did not go on the cruise.
Clue No. 3 and **Clue No. 1** tell us that Oscar did not go to the seashore.
Clue No. 4 tells us that neither Kimberly nor Nicole went to the theme park.
Clue No. 5 tells us that neither Hector nor Oscar went to the seashore and that a boy went to the theme park.
Clue No. 5 and **Clue No. 2** tell us Kimberly did not go to the seashore; therefore, Nicole went to the seashore.
Clue No. 6 tells us that a girl went on the cruise and a boy went to the mountains; therefore, Kimberly went on the cruise. Because Hector does not come after Kimberly alphabetically, we know that Hector did not go to the mountains; therefore, Oscar went to the mountains and Hector went to the theme park.

Who Won the Race?
Clue No. 1 tells us Jackson's last name is Leary.
Clue No. 2 tells us Ryan's last name is not Silver.
Clue No. 3 tells us Ava's last name is Gold or Silver.
Clue No. 4 tells us a girl is named Gold and that Elyssa is not named Gold. We now know that Ava is named Gold. We also know Elyssa is named Silver and Ryan is named Thomas.
Clue No. 5 tells us there are 4 letters in the winner's first name, so Ryan Thomas won the race.

The Case of the Muddy Carpet
Clue No. 1 tells us that neither Candy nor Samantha is 40.
Clue No. 2 tells us that Candy is 10.

© **Barbara M. Peller**

Clue No. 3 and Clue No. 1 tell us that Rocky is not 40. We now know that Tom is 40.

Clue No. 4 tells us that Samantha is not 8. We now know that Samantha is 4 and Rocky is 8.

With Clue No. 2 we now know that Samantha muddied the carpet.

Feline : Cat :: Canine : <u>Dog</u>   Samantha is a <u>dog</u>.

LEVEL 2 MYSTERIES

Precious Pet Parade

Clue No. 2 and Clue No. 1 tell us that Lisa was 9 and did not enter the iguana.

Clue No. 3 and Clue No. 2 tell us that neither Hunter nor Joey entered the iguana. We now know that Maria entered the iguana. We now know Maria is 6, Joey is 8, Hunter is 7, and Lisa is 9.

Clue No. 4 and Clue No. 3 tell us that neither Joey nor Hunter entered the dog. We now know that Lisa is the one who entered the dog.

Clue No. 5 tells us that Joey entered the bunny; therefore, Hunter entered the cat.

Syllogism: <u>Therefore, the bunny, the cat, and the dog did not win the prize for most unusual pet.</u>

Conclusion: <u>The iguana won the prize.</u>

The Case of the Melted Ice Cream

Clue No. 2 tells us Matt and Jeff did not eat the ice cream and Liz and Kate did not eat the apple.

Clue No. 4 tells us Jeff did not have the cookies and a girl did; therefore, we also know Matt did not.

Clue No. 5 tells us Kate had the cookies. We now also know Liz had the ice cream.

Clue No. 7 and Clue No. 6 tell us Jeff ate the sandwich. We also know that Matt ate the apple.

With Clue No. 3 we know Liz left out the ice cream.

Who Opened Tweety's Cage?

Clue No. 2 tells us that Liam was not in the backyard.

Clue No. 3 tells us Danny and Tom were not in the bedroom.

Clue No. 4 tells us Sammy and Danny were not in the dining room.

Clue No. 5 and Clue No. 1 tell us that Sammy was in the bedroom and Danny was in the backyard.

Clue No. 6 tells us that Liam was in the dining room. We now also know that Tom was in the kitchen. From the story we also know that Tom opened the cage door.

TOM - <u>TOT</u> - <u>COT</u> - **CAT**   Tom is a <u>cat</u>.

The Case of the Potted Plant

Clue No. 1 tells us that neither Tigger nor Spot is the dog.

Clue No. 2 tells us that Tigger is not the guinea pig.

Clue No. 3 tells us that Tigger is not the parrot.
We now know that Tigger is the cat.

Clue No. 4 tells us that Penny is the parrot. We now know Max is the dog and Spot is the guinea pig.

fish : fins :: **bird** : feathers
A **bird** knocked over the plant!
Alliteration is the type of figurative language used.

Who Wrote the Note?

Clue No. 1 tells us Jane Brook does not live on First and whoever is her cousin does.

Clue No. 3 tells us Jane Jordan doesn't live on First or Lincoln.

Clue No. 4 tells us Jane Jordan does not live on Main; therefore, she lives on Central. With Clue No. 2 we know Jane Lewis does not live on Main.

Clue No. 5 tells us that Jane Lewis does not live on First because neither Brook nor Canby comes after Lewis alphabetically; therefore, Jane Canby lives on First. We now know Jane Lewis lives on Lincoln and Jane Brook lives on Main.

Clue No. 6 and Clue No. 1 tell us Jane Brook wrote it.

NOTE - <u>NATE</u> - <u>LATE</u> - <u>LAKE</u> - <u>BAKE</u> - <u>BIKE</u>
Jane wanted to show her a <u>bike</u>.

Working for a Good Cause

Clue No. 2 and Clue No. 1 tell us that Jim did not clean up or sell food.

Clue No. 4 and Clue No. 3 tell us Jamal sold tickets. We now know that Jim sold shirts.

Clue No. 5 tells us that Josh did not sell food. We now know that Jake sold food. We also know that Josh cleaned up.

Clue No. 6 tells us that Jim won the prize.

A Trip to the Zoo

Clue No. 1 tells us that Nick did not draw an elephant.

Clue No. 4, Clue No. 2 and Clue No. 3 tell us neither Nick nor Amanda drew a lamb or a tiger. We now know Nick drew the giraffe and Amanda drew the elephant.

Clue No. 5 and Clue No. 4 tell us April is the oldest child. With Clue No. 2 we know that April drew the lamb. We now also know that Ashley drew the tiger.

OMNEYK = <u>MONKEY</u> (Most Popular Animal)

Who Took Grandma's Laptop?

Clue No. 1 tells us that Sophia is not Ruth's granddaughter or granddaughter's friend.

Clue No. 2 tells us Lauren is not Ruth's granddaughter. Because we know Ruth's granddaughter is only ten, we know Lauren is her granddaughter's friend.

Clue No. 4 tells us Rachel was in the living room.

Clue No. 5 tells us Sophia is Ruth's sister. We now also know that Rachel is her daughter and Olivia is her granddaughter.

Clue No. 6 tells us the person who took the laptop was in the dining room. With Clue No. 3 and Clue No. 4 we know Sophia and Lauren were in the kitchen and Rachel was in the living room; therefore, Olivia was in the dining room. We now know Olivia, her granddaughter, took the laptop.

Who Rang the Doorbell?

Clue No. 2 tells us that Cameron did not say he was in the bookstore. We also know he is 10.

Clue No. 3 tells us Mario is not 9; therefore, he is 12. We also know Cole and Nathan are the twins. With **Clue No. 2** we know Mario said he was in the bookstore.

Clue No. 4 tells us that neither Cole nor Nathan said he was in the supermarket. We now know that Cameron said he was in the supermarket.

Clue No. 5 tells us that Cole did not say he was at the library. We now know that Nathan said he was at the library and Cole said he was at the zoo.

$10 + 12 + 9 + 9 = 40 \quad 40 \div 4 = 10$

The average age is 10, so Cameron rang the bell.

The Case of the Broken Vase

Clue No. 2 tells us that Angie is not the babysitter.

Clue No. 3 tells us that the babysitter is female; therefore, neither Rick nor Tyler is the babysitter. We now know Samantha is the babysitter.

Clue No. 3 also tells us that the babysitter was in the library. We now know Samantha was in the library.

Clue No. 4 tells us Rick was not in the living room. It also tells us the person in the living room is female; therefore, we know Tyler was not in the living room. We now know that Angie was in the living room.

Clue No. 5 tells us that Tyler was on the deck. We now also know that Rick was in the kitchen.

The location of the vase is needed.

Message: <u>The vase was in the kitchen.</u>

LEVEL 3 MYSTERIES

The Case of the Missing Pie

With the introduction and **Clue No. 1** we know Samuel, Logan, and Mike cannot be her daughter or friend of her daughter; Brooke and Ellie are not her husband, son, or friend of her son.

Clue No. 2 tells us that Dad is 45. Neither girl is 45.

Clue No. 3 tells us that the females have to be 16 and 17. and none of the males are 16 or 17.

Clue No. 4 tells us Mike is 15 and not her husband.

Clue No. 5 tells us Mike is not her son and Ellie is not her daughter. We now know Ellie is her daughter's friend and Brooke is her daughter. We also know Mike is her son's friend.

Clue No. 6 tells us Logan is her son and that he is 14. We now also know Samuel is her husband and is 45. We know Brooke is 16 and Ellie is 17.

$4 (6 + 2) - 18 = \underline{14}$ Therefore, Logan ate Mom's pie.

The Case of the Missing Library Book

Clue No. 1 tells us Mr. Green is not the police officer.

Clue No. 2 tells us that neither Mr. Write nor Miss Nicely is the dentist.

Clue No. 3 tells us that Miss Saturn is the dentist.

Clue No. 4 and **Clue No. 1** tell us Miss January is not the

police officer.

Clue No. 5 tells us Mr. Write is not the author or police officer. We now know Miss Nicely is the police officer.

Clue No. 6 tells us that Mr. Green is the teacher. We now know that Mr. Write is the banker and Miss January is the author.

Message: <u>The author took the book to sign it!</u>

Who Woke Grandpa?

Clue No. 1 tells us neither Megan nor Alanna is blond.

Clue No. 2 tells us neither Dylan nor Aidan has red hair.

Clue No. 3 tells us that Megan has red hair.

Clue No. 3 and **Clue No. 2** tell us that Megan was in the kitchen.

Clue No. 4 tells us neither Alanna nor Dylan has black hair. We now know Aidan has black hair. We also know Dylan has blond hair, and Alanna has brown hair.

With **Clue No. 1** we know Dylan was in the dining room.

Clue No. 5 tells us that a girl was in the living room; therefore, we know that Alanna was in the living room. We also know that Aidan was in the bedroom; therefore, he woke Grandpa.

A Group Project

Clue No. 1 tells us Jackson and Oliver did not get paint.

Clue No. 2 tells us that Ruth, Sadie, and Meg did not get the colored paper.

Clue No. 3 tells us Jackson did not get the poster board or colored pencils. It also tells us that Ruth, Sadie, and Meg did not get the colored pencils. We now know that Oliver got the colored pencils. We now know Jackson got the colored paper.

Clue No. 5 tells us that Ruth did not get the glue.

Clue No. 6 tells us that Meg did not get the poster board or the paint.

Clue No. 7 tells us Meg got the glue and the scissors.

Clue No. 8 tells us Ruth did not get the poster board; therefore, she got the paint and Sadie got the poster board.

A Costume Contest

Clue No. 1 tells us that the robot took the school bus.

Clue No. 2 tells us that Alyssa was not the unicorn.

Clue No. 3 tells us a boy won for Funniest Costume. We now know neither Alyssa nor Abigail won for Funniest Costume.

Clue No. 4 tells us that Carlos was not Abe Lincoln. Because a boy was Lincoln, Karl was Abe Lincoln.

Clue No. 5 tells us that a girl was dressed as an astronaut and that she won for Most Original Costume. We now know Carlos was not the astronaut and neither Carlos nor Karl won for Most Original.

Clue No. 6 tells us that Karl won for Most Accurate Costume. We now know that Carlos won for Funniest Costume.

Clue No. 7 tells us that Abigail did not win for Most Original Costume; therefore, Alyssa won for Most Original and Abigail for Cutest.

© **Barbara M. Peller**

Clue No. 7 and Clue No. 5 tell us that Alyssa was the astronaut. Because we know that Alyssa won for Most Original Costume, we now know that she, Karl, and Abigail walked to school together. With Clue No. 1, we know Carlos was the robot. We now also know Abigail was the unicorn.

Who Played What?

Clue No. 1 tells us only one child plays an instrument whose name begins with the letter of his or her name.

Clue No. 2 and information in the story tell us 2 fifth graders had a solo.

Clue No. 3 tells us Heather does not play the drums and one of the fifth graders does.

Clue No. 4 tells us that Summer is the violinist.

Clue No. 5 tells us that Summer had a solo.

Clue No. 6 tells us that Conner plays the cello.

Clue No. 6 and Clue No. 1 tell us that Frank does not play the flute.

Clue No. 7 tells us that there are only 2 fifth graders and we know that both had a solo.

Clue No. 8 tells us Lacy did not play the flute and that a girl played the flute. We now know that Heather played the flute.

Clue No. 9 tells us Frank is in the fourth grade. With Clue No. 3 we know that he did not play the drums; therefore, Lacy played the drums; we also know that she was in the fifth grade and had the other solo. We also know Frank played the trumpet.

The Case of the Open Door

Clue No. 1 tells us that his wife and sister are 34 and 36 and that his mother is 70.

Clue No. 2 tells us that Barbara is not his daughter. We now know that Barbara is his niece and is 15.

Clue No. 3 and Clue No. 1 tell us that Taylor is not 70. We now know that Taylor is not his mother.

Clue No. 4 tells us Mr. Costa and his sister are the same age.

Clue No. 5 tells us Taylor did not leave the door open.

Clue No. 6 tells us Melissa is his daughter and is 12.

Clue No. 7 tells us that Anna is his wife. We now know Taylor is his sister and Sofia is his mother and is 70.

Clue No. 8 tells us that Anna is 34 and Taylor is 36.

Solve the problem: 10 + 10 + 8 + 8 = 36

The person who left it open is 36. Taylor is 36, but we know from Clue No. 4 that Mr. Costa and Taylor were twins. We know from Clue No. 5 that Taylor did not leave the door open; therefore, Mr. Costa left it open!

The Case of the Missing Project

Clue No. 1 tells us that Isabella did not write the poem and did not chose Dr. Seuss.

Clue No. 2 tells us that neither Becca nor Emily chose Thomas Edison. Because a boy chose Thomas Edison, we also know that Isabella did not choose him.

Clue No. 3 tells us that neither Eric nor Neil wrote a song. (One of them could have chosen a President.)

Clue No. 4 tells us that Becca did not chose George Washington and that she did not do a painting.

Clue No. 5 tells us that Becca wrote the report.

Clue No. 6, Clue No. 3, and Clue No. 4 tell us that Emily wrote a song about Abraham Lincoln.

Clue No. 7 tells us Becca wrote a report about Sacajawea. We now know Isabella chose George Washington and with Clue No. 4 that she made a painting.

Clue No. 8 tells us that Eric made a poster about Thomas Edison. We also know that Neil wrote a poem about Dr. Seuss.

Paintings : Art Gallery :: Books : Library

The project is on display in the library.

Celebrating America Song Festival

Clue No. 4 tells us that Grade 5 is taught by Mr. Allan or Mr. Ray.

Clue No. 5 tells us that Mr. Allan teaches Grade 1. We now know that Mr. Ray teaches Grade 5.

Clue No. 6 and Clue No. 2 tell us that Grade 1 sang "Yankee Doodle Dandy."

Clue No. 7 tells us that Grade 1 and Grade 2 did not sing "The Star-Spangled Banner."

Clue No. 8 tells us that Mrs. Cape teaches Grade 3.

Clue No. 9 tells us that either Grade 4 or Grade 5 sang "America the Beautiful."

Clue No. 10 tells us that Grade 5 sang "This Land Is Your Land." With Clue No. 9 we know Grade 4 sang "America the Beautiful. We also know that Grade 2 sang "You're a Grand Old Flag," and Grade 3 sang "The Star-Spangled Banner."

Clue No. 11 tells us that Miss Green does not teach Grade 2. We now know that Miss Green teaches Grade 4 and Mrs. Arms teaches Grade 2.

Message: The names are in alphabetical order.

Pen Pals

Clue No. 2 tells us Charlotte's pen pal lives in North Carolina.

Clue No. 3 tells us only Ava's or Elle's pen pal can be named Madison.

Clue No. 4 tells us Savannah does not live in Georgia. With Clue No. 1 we now know that Austin lives in Texas and Madison lives in Wisconsin.

Clue No. 5 tells us Ava's pen pal lives in Georgia. With Clue No. 3 we now know Madison is Elle's pen pal.

Clue No. 6 tells us Savannah is Charlotte's pen pal. We now know Savannah lives in North Carolina.

Clue No. 7 tells us Otto's pen pal lives in Texas; therefore, Otto's pen pal is named Austin. We also know Juan lives in California.

Clue No. 8 tells us May does not live in California; therefore, she lives in Georgia. We now know that May is Ava's pen pal. We also know that Gary is Juan's pen pal and that he lives in California.

© Barbara M. Peller

Solution for Scoops for You

	1 Scoop	2 Scoops	3 Scoops	Sundae
Becca	✗	✗	✔	✗
Eli	✗	✔	✗	✗
Jennie	✔	✗	✗	✗
Carolina	✗	✗	✗	✔

Becca ordered three scoops .
Eli ordered two scoops .
Jennie ordered one scoop .
Carolina ordered the sundae .

Solution for Which Sport?

	Soccer	Basketball	Baseball	Field Hockey
Ethan	✗	✗	✔	✗
Jacob	✗	✔	✗	✗
Andrew	✗	✗	✗	✔
Austin	✔	✗	✗	✗

Ethan favors baseball.
Jacob favors basketball.
Andrew favors field hockey.
Austin favors soccer.

Solution for A Foul-Shooting Competition

	Apple	Black	Green	Rose	17	19	20	23
Brad	✔	✗	✗	✗	✗	✔	✗	✗
Justin	✗	✗	✗	✔	✔	✗	✗	✗
Rebecca	✗	✗	✔	✗	✗	✗	✗	✔
Zack	✗	✔	✗	✗	✗	✗	✔	✗

Brad Apple made 19 shots.
Justin Rose made 17 shots.
Rebecca Green made 23 shots.
Zack Black made 20 shots.
Rebecca won the competition.

Solution for Town Fair Puzzle Contest

	Grades K-2	Grades 3-5	Grades 6-8	Grades 9-12
Scarlet	✔	✗	✗	✗
Brianna	✗	✔	✗	✗
Jimmy	✗	✗	✔	✗
Rebecca	✗	✗	✗	✔

Scarlet was the winner of the Grades K–2 Group.
Brianna was the winner of the Grades 3–5 Group.
Jimmy was the winner of the Grades 6–8 Group.
Rebecca was the winner of the Grades 9–12 Group.

Solution for Works of Art

	Playground Fun	Animal Babies	Jungle Scene	A Day at the Beach	50	50	100	300
Scarlet (K-2)	✗	✔	✗	✗	✔			
Brianna (3-5)	✔	✗	✗	✗		✔		
Jimmy (6-8)	✗	✗	✔	✗			✔	
Rebecca (9-12)	✗	✗	✗	✔				✔

Scarlet's puzzle work of art: "Animal Babies."
Brianna's puzzle work of art: "Playground Fun."
Jimmy's puzzle work of art; "Jungle Scene."
Rebecca's puzzle work of art: "A Day at the Beach."

Solution for Choose a Cupcake

	Cookie Pieces	Chocolate Chips	Rainbow Sprinkles	Coconut Flakes
Sara	✗	✗	✔	✗
Ella	✔	✗	✗	✗
Lily	✗	✗	✗	✔
Isabella	✗	✔	✗	✗

Sara chose the rainbow sprinkles.
Ella chose the cookie pieces.
Lily chose the coconut flakes.
Isabella chose the chocolate chips.

© Barbara M. Peller

Solution for A Day at the Circus

	Clowns	Acrobats	Jugglers	Tightrope Walker
Annie	✗	✗	✓	✗
Bob	✗	✗	✗	✓
Mom	✓	✗	✗	✗
Dad	✗	✓	✗	✗

Annie liked the jugglers.
Bob liked the tightrope walker.
Mom liked the clowns.
Dad liked the acrobats.
STRANGER Mom Annie Bob Dad AISLE

Solution for Vacation Fun

	Seashore	Mountain Resort	Cruise	Theme Park
Hector	✗	✗	✗	✓
Oscar	✗	✓	✗	✗
Nicole	✓	✗	✗	✗
Kimberly	✗	✗	✓	✗

Hector went to the theme park.
Oscar went to the mountain resort.
Nicole went to the seashore.
Kimberly went on a cruise.

Solution for Who Won the Race?

	Gold	Silver	Thomas	Leary
Elyssa	✗	✓	✗	✗
Ava	✓	✗	✗	✗
Ryan	✗	✗	✓	✗
Jackson	✗	✗	✗	✓

Elyssa Silver
Ava Gold
Ryan Thomas
Jackson Leary
Ryan Thomas ran the fastest.

Solution for The Case of the Muddy Carpet

	4	8	10	40
Rocky	✗	✓	✗	✗
Samantha	✓	✗	✗	✗
Candy	✗	✗	✓	✗
Tom	✗	✗	✗	✓

Rocky is 8 years old.
Samantha is 4 years old.
Candy is 10 years old.
Tom is 40 years old.
Samantha muddied the carpet!
The one who muddied the carpet is a dog.

Solution for Precious Pet Parade

	Dog	Bunny	Cat	Iguana	6	7	8	9
Lisa	✓	✗	✗	✗	✗	✗	✗	✓
Joey	✗	✓	✗	✗	✗	✗	✓	✗
Hunter	✗	✗	✓	✗	✗	✓	✗	✗
Maria	✗	✗	✗	✓	✓	✗	✗	✗

Lisa is 9 and entered a dog.
Joey is 8 and entered a bunny.
Hunter is 7 and entered a cat.
Maria is 6 and entered an iguana.
Maria won the prize for Most Unusual Pet.

Solution for Case of the Melted Ice Cream

	P. B. & J Sandwich	Cookies	Apple	Ice Cream
Liz	✗	✗	✗	✓
Kate	✗	✓	✗	✗
Matt	✗	✗	✓	✗
Jeff	✓	✗	✗	✗

Liz had ice cream.
Kate had cookies.
Matt had an apple.
Jake had a peanut butter and jelly sandwich.
Liz left the ice cream on the counter.

Solution for Who Opened Tweety's Cage?

	Kitchen	Bedroom	Dining Room	Backyard
Sammy	✗	✔	✗	✗
Liam	✗	✗	✔	✗
Tom	✔	✗	✗	✗
Danny	✗	✗	✗	✔

Sammy was in the <u>bedroom.</u>
Liam was in the <u>dining room.</u>
Tom was in the <u>kitchen.</u>
Danny was in the <u>backyard.</u>
<u>Tom</u> left the cage door open.
TOM ⟿ <u>TOT</u> ⟿ <u>COT</u> ⟿ <u>CAT</u>   Tom is a <u>cat.</u>

Solution for Who Wrote the Note?

	Main	Central	First	Lincoln
Canby	✗	✗	✔	✗
Jordan	✗	✔	✗	✗
Brook	✔	✗	✗	✗
Lewis	✗	✗	✗	✔

Jane Canby lived on <u>First.</u>
Jane Jordan lived on <u>Central.</u>
Jane Brook lived on <u>Main.</u>
Jane Lewis lived on <u>Lincoln.</u>
<u>Jane Brook</u> wrote the note.
NOTE ⟿ <u>NATE</u> ⟿ <u>LATE</u> ⟿ <u>LAKE</u> ⟿ <u>BAKE</u> ⟿ <u>BIKE</u>
She wanted to show Jessica a <u>bike.</u>

Solution for A Trip to the Zoo

	Giraffe	Elephant	Lamb	Tiger
Amanda	✗	✔	✗	✗
Nick	✔	✗	✗	✗
April	✗	✗	✔	✗
Ashley	✗	✗	✗	✔

Amanda drew <u>an elephant.</u>
Nick drew <u>a giraffe.</u>
April drew <u>a lamb.</u>
Ashley drew <u>a tiger.</u>
The <u>monkey</u> was the most popular choice.

Solution for Case of the Potted Plant

	Dog	Cat	Guinea Pig	Parrot
Max	✔	✗	✗	✗
Penny	✗	✗	✗	✔
Spot	✗	✗	✔	✗
Tigger	✗	✔	✗	✗

Max is a <u>dog.</u>
Penny is a <u>parrot.</u>
Spot is a <u>guinea pig.</u>
Tigger is a <u>cat.</u>
fish : fins :: bird : <u>cat</u>
The <u>cat (Tigger)</u> knocked over the plant.
<u>Alliteration</u> was the type of figurative language used.

Solution for Working for a Good Cause

	Food	Tickets	Shirts	Clean-up
Jim	✗	✗	✔	✗
Jake	✔	✗	✗	✗
Jamal	✗	✔	✗	✗
Josh	✗	✗	✗	✔

Jim was on the <u>Shirts</u> Committee.
Jake was on the <u>Food</u> Committee.
Jamal was on the <u>Tickets</u> Committee.
Josh was on the <u>Clean-up</u> Committee.
<u>Jim</u> won the prize.

Solution for Who Took Grandma's Laptop?

	Sister	Daughter	Granddaughter	Friend of Granddaughter
Rachel	✗	✔	✗	✗
Lauren	✗	✗	✗	✔
Olivia	✗	✗	✔	✗
Sophia	✔	✗	✗	✗

Rachel was <u>Grandma Ruth's daughter.</u>
Lauren was <u>a friend of Grandma Ruth's granddaughter.</u>
Olivia was <u>Grandma Ruth's granddaughter.</u>
Sophia was <u>Grandma Ruth's sister.</u>
<u>Olivia</u> took the laptop.

© Barbara M. Peller

Solution for Who Rang the Doorbell?

	Library	Supermarket	Zoo	bookstore
Cole	✗	✗	✔	✗
Mario	✗	✗	✗	✔
Nathan	✔	✗	✗	✗
Cameron	✗	✔	✗	✗

Cole said he was at the <u>zoo</u>.
Mario said he was at the <u>bookstore</u>.
Nathan said he was at the <u>library</u>.
Cameron said he was at the <u>supermarket</u>.
The average age of the boys was <u>10</u>.
<u>Cameron</u> rang the bell.

Solution for The Case of the Missing Pie

	14	15	16	17	45	Husband	Daughter	Son	Friend of Daughter	Friend of Son
Samuel	✗	✗	✗	✗	✔	✔	✗	✗	✗	✗
Brooke	✗	✗	✔	✗	✗	✗	✔	✗	✗	✗
Ellie	✗	✗	✗	✔	✗	✗	✗	✗	✔	✗
Logan	✔	✗	✗	✗	✗	✗	✗	✔	✗	✗
Mike	✗	✔	✗	✗	✗	✗	✗	✗	✗	✔

Samuel was <u>45</u> years old.   <u>Husband</u>
Brooke was <u>16</u> years old.   <u>Daughter</u>
Ellie was <u>17</u> years old.   <u>Friend of Daughter</u>
Logan was <u>14</u> years old.   <u>Son</u>
Michael was <u>15</u> years old.   <u>Friend of Son</u>
$4(6+2) - 18 = \underline{14}$ <u>Logan</u> ate Mom's pie.

Solution for Who Woke Grandpa?

	Kitchen	Living Room	Dining Room	Bedroom	Brown	Black	Blond	Red
Alanna	✗	✔	✗	✗	✔	✗	✗	✗
Dylan	✗	✗	✔	✗	✗	✗	✔	✗
Megan	✔	✗	✗	✗	✗	✗	✗	✔
Aidan	✗	✗	✗	✔	✗	✔	✗	✗

Alanna was in the <u>living room</u>.   <u>brown</u> hair.
Dylan was in the <u>dining room</u>.   <u>blond</u> hair.
Megan was in the <u>kitchen</u>.   <u>red</u> hair.
Aidan was in the <u>bedroom</u>.   <u>black</u> hair.
<u>Aidan</u> woke Grandpa.

Solution for The Case of the Broken Vase

	Kitchen	Living Room	Library	Deck
Samantha	✗	✗	✔	✗
Tyler	✗	✗	✗	✔
Rick	✔	✗	✗	✗
Angie	✗	✔	✗	✗

Samantha was <u>in the library</u>.
Tyler was <u>on the deck</u>.
Rick was <u>in the kitchen</u>.
Angie was <u>in the living room</u>.
MESSAGE: <u>The vase was in the kitchen</u>.
<u>Rick</u> knocked over the vase.

Solution for Case of the Missing Library Book

	Police Officer	Dentist	Author	Banker	Teacher
Mr. Green	✗	✗	✗	✗	✔
Miss Nicely	✔	✗	✗	✗	✗
Miss January	✗	✗	✔	✗	✗
Miss Saturn	✗	✔	✗	✗	✗
Mr. Write	✗	✗	✗	✔	✗

Mr. Green is <u>a teacher</u>.
Miss Nicely is <u>a police officer</u>.
Miss January is <u>an author</u>.
Miss Saturn is <u>a dentist</u>.
Mr. Write is <u>a banker</u>.
MESSAGE: <u>The author took the book to sign it</u>.
<u>Miss January</u> took the book.

Solution for A Group Project

	Colored Pencils	Poster Board	Paint	Colored Paper	Glue	Scissors
Oliver	✔	✗	✗	✗	✗	✗
Ruth	✗	✗	✔	✗	✗	✗
Sadie	✗	✔	✗	✗	✗	✗
Jackson	✗	✗	✗	✔	✗	✗
Michele	✗	✗	✗	✗	✔	✔

Oliver agreed to get the <u>colored pencils</u>.
Ruth agreed to get the <u>paint</u>.
Sadie agreed to get the <u>poster board</u>.
Jackson agreed to get the <u>colored paper</u>.
Michele agreed to get the <u>glue and scissors</u>.

Solution for A Costume Contest

	Astronaut	Abraham Lincoln	Robot	Unicorn	Cutest	Original	Accurate	Funniest
Matthew	✗	✓	✗	✗	✗	✗	✓	✗
Carlos	✗	✗	✓	✗	✗	✗	✗	✓
Abigail	✗	✗	✗	✓	✓	✗	✗	✗
Alyssa	✓	✗	✗	✗	✗	✓	✗	✗

Matthew was dressed as Abraham Lincoln and won Most Accurate.
Carlos was dressed as a robot and won Funniest.
Abigail was dressed as a unicorn and won Cutest.
Alyssa was dressed as an astronaut and won Most Original.

Solution for Who Played What?

	Violin	Cello	Trumpet	Flute	Drums
Lacy	✗	✗	✗	✗	✓
Heather	✗	✗	✗	✓	✗
Frank	✗	✗	✓	✗	✗
Summer	✓	✗	✗	✗	✗
Conner	✗	✓	✗	✗	✗

Lacy played the drums.
Heather played the flute.
Frank played the trumpet.
Summer played the violin.
Conner played the cello.
Lacy and Summer had solos.

Solution for The Case of the Open Door

	Wife	Mother	Sister	Daughter	Niece	12	15	36	34	70
Anna	✓	✗	✗	✗	✗	✗	✗	✗	✓	✗
Barbara	✗	✗	✗	✗	✓	✗	✓	✗	✗	✗
Melissa	✗	✗	✗	✓	✗	✓	✗	✗	✗	✗
Sofia	✗	✓	✗	✗	✗	✗	✗	✗	✗	✓
Teresa	✗	✗	✓	✗	✗	✗	✗	✓	✗	✗

Anna is Mr. Costa's wife and is 34 years old.
Barbara is Mr. Costa's niece and is 15 years old.
Melissa is Mr. Costa's daughter and is 12 years old.
Sofia is Mr. Costa's mother and is 70 years old.
Taylor is Mr. Costa's sister and is 36 years old.
The person who left the door open is 36 years old.
Mr. Costa left the door open.

Solution for Case of the Missing Project

	George Washington	Abraham Lincoln	Dr. Seuss	Thomas Edison	Sacajawea	Painting	Poster	Report	Poem	Song
Neil	✗	✗	✓	✗	✗	✗	✗	✗	✓	✗
Isabella	✓	✗	✗	✗	✗	✓	✗	✗	✗	✗
Eric	✗	✗	✗	✓	✗	✗	✓	✗	✗	✗
Becca	✗	✗	✗	✗	✓	✗	✗	✓	✗	✗
Emily	✗	✓	✗	✗	✗	✗	✗	✗	✗	✓

Neil's project was a poem about Dr. Seuss.
Isabella's project was a painting of George Washington.
Eric's project was a poster about Thomas Edison.
Becca's project was a report about Sacajawea.
Emily's project was a song about Abraham Lincoln.
Neil's project was missing.
It was on display in the library.

Solution for Celebrating Amer. Song Festival

	Mrs. Arms	Mrs. Cape	Miss Green	Mr. Allan	Mr. Ray	Star-Spangled Banner	Yankee Doodle Dandy	You're a Grand Old Flag	America the Beautiful	This Land Is Your Land
Grade 1	✗	✗	✗	✓	✗	✗	✓	✗	✗	✗
Grade 2	✓	✗	✗	✗	✗	✗	✗	✓	✗	✗
Grade 3	✗	✓	✗	✗	✗	✓	✗	✗	✗	✗
Grade 4	✗	✗	✓	✗	✗	✗	✗	✗	✓	✗
Grade 5	✗	✗	✗	✗	✓	✗	✗	✗	✗	✓

Grade 1   Mr. Allan   "Yankee Doodle Dandy"
Grade 2   Mrs. Arms   "You're a Grand Old Flag"
Grade 3   Mrs. Cape   "The Star-Spangled Banner."
Grade 4   Mr. Green   "America the Beautiful"
Grade 5   Mr. Ray   "This Land Is Your Land"
Message: The names are in alphabetical order.

Solution for Pen Pals

	CA	GA	NC	TX	WI	Madison	Austin	Savannah	Gary	May
Juan	✓	✗	✗	✗	✗	✗	✗	✗	✓	✗
Elle	✗	✗	✗	✗	✓	✓	✗	✗	✗	✗
Hannah	✗	✓	✗	✗	✗	✗	✗	✗	✗	✓
Otto	✗	✗	✗	✓	✗	✗	✓	✗	✗	✗
Charlotte	✗	✗	✓	✗	✗	✗	✗	✓	✗	✗

	CA	GA	NC	TX	WI	Juan	Elle	Hannah	Otto	Charlotte
Madison	✗	✗	✗	✗	✓	✗	✓	✗	✗	✗
Austin	✗	✗	✗	✓	✗	✗	✗	✗	✓	✗
Savannah	✗	✗	✓	✗	✗	✗	✗	✗	✗	✓
Gary	✓	✗	✗	✗	✗	✓	✗	✗	✗	✗
May	✗	✓	✗	✗	✗	✗	✗	✓	✗	✗

Juan's pen pal is named Gary and lives in California.
Elle's pen pal is named Madison and lives in Wisconsin.
Hannah's pen pal is named May and lives in Georgia.
Otto's pen pal is named Austin and lives in Texas.
Charlotte's pen pal is named Savannah and lives in North Carolina.

© Barbara M. Peller

www.ingramcontent.com/pod-product-compliance
Lightning Source LLC
Chambersburg PA
CBHW081237090426
42738CB00016B/3335